Your Child's Baptism

Revised Edition

Paul Turner

LITURGY
TRAINING
PUBLICATIONS

D1472568

Nihil Obstat
Reverend Mr. Daniel G. Welter, JD
Chancellor
Archdiocese of Chicago
November 14, 2017

Imprimatur
Very Reverend Ronald A. Hicks
Vicar General
Archdiocese of Chicago
November 14, 2017

The *Nihil Obstat* and *Imprimatur* are declarations that the material is free from doctrinal or moral error, and thus is granted permission to publish in accordance with c. 827. No legal responsibility is assumed by the grant of this permission. No implication is contained herein that those who have granted the *Nihil Obstat* and *Imprimatur* agree with the content, opinions, or statements expressed.

YOUR CHILD'S BAPTISM © 2018 Archdiocese of Chicago: Liturgy Training Publications, 3949 South Racine Avenue, Chicago, IL 60609; 800-933-1800; fax 800-933-7094; e-mail: orders@ltp.org; website: www.LTP.org. All rights reserved.

This book was edited by Lorie Simmons. Víctor R. Pérez was the production editor, Anna Manhart was the designer, and Luis Leal was the production artist.

Cover Photo © John Zich.

Interior photos: Pages iii, iv, 8, 14, and 33 © Carolyn and Nick Manhart; pages 24, 27 © LTP; page 28 © Emily Reynolds TheTulipPatch.etsycom; pages iv, 15, 18, and 29 © John Zich; pages iii, 1, 6, and 26 © Maria Laughlin.

22 21 20 19 18   1 2 3 4 5

Printed in the United States of America.

ISBN 978-1-61671-419-2

CHBAPTR

CONTENTS

INTRODUCTION TO THE
REVISED EDITION

In the years since I wrote the first edition of this book, I have lost my parents, my godparents, and the priest who baptized me at Our Lady of Lourdes Catholic Church in New Orleans, Louisiana, when I was three days old. If anything, those years have filled me with a greater awareness of the generous love that parents give their children. The sacrifice that others made on my behalf humbles me. I would not be serving as a priest today, nor would I have written a book such as this, if I had not received the loving care of those closest to me at the beginning of my life.

To you, the parent reading this book, I offer my esteem, appreciation, and gratitude. You have welcomed a child into your home with a deep desire to share your love. You want this child to have the best the world can offer, and that includes the gift of Baptism, life in Christ, and participation in his Body, the Church. The way you open your arms to your child challenges others to open their hearts as well. You want to make the world a better place, and the power of the Holy Spirit will be with you.

A child inconveniences a parent. A growingly independent child tests a parent's love. I harbor doubts when I ask parents this question near the beginning of the baptismal ceremony: "Do you clearly understand what you are undertaking?" No parents clearly understand what they are undertaking, but they always answer, "We do." That brief statement testifies to their faith and love, and it always leaves me slack-jawed.

The revised edition of this book has cleared up a few points of Church practice and acknowledges new contemporary challenges. I hope that it will not only help you celebrate your child's Baptism, but renew your commitment to Christ and the Church.

I also pray that one day your child will come to a deeper awareness of the meaning of this day. I pray that you may live to hear this child render generous thanks to you for all your love and sacrifice. Until then, please accept my admiration and gratitude, as a fellow citizen of the world and member of the Body of Christ.

CHECKLIST

○ Find out if your parish celebrates Baptism at Mass, or apart from Mass.

○ Find out if your parish has a list of days on which Baptism is celebrated.

○ Learn the words to say in case you need to perform an emergency Baptism.

○ Talk with the godparents about their responsibilities.

○ Attend the parish Baptism preparation sessions.

○ Give instructions to photographers.

○ Prepare your response to the question, "What do you ask of God's Church for your child?"

○ Decide what garment your child will wear to, during, and after the Baptism.

○ If your child is wearing a garment that fits close to the neck, be sure it can be loosened if the minister anoints the breast with the oil of catechumens.

○ Decide whether to have your child baptized by immersion or by pouring.

○ Find out if the church will furnish the baptismal candle. If you will be providing the candle, be sure it's ready before the ceremony.

○ If you want to carry holy water home after the Baptism, bring a small container.

○ Plan the party.

○ Consider offering a gift to your parish.

○ Register as a member of your parish.

CHAPTER 1

Parents and Children

Congratulations! God has blessed you with a child! And now you are presenting that child for Baptism in the Catholic Church. All of us who share faith with you rejoice. You have accepted a new life into your home, a child who will grace our world. Now through the mystery of Baptism that child will be born again.

This Baptism will mean a lot for your child, for you, and for the community. Through Baptism, that youngster will become a disciple, part of the Body of Christ. Through Baptism, you affirm that you will raise your child in the practice of the faith. Through Baptism, our community is enriched with one who will grow in faith, share our concerns, serve others, and join us in the praise of God.

Here are some preparatory considerations for you.

The Age of Your Child

A child should generally be baptized within the first few weeks after birth (*Code of Canon Law*, 867 §1). The Baptism does not have to happen right away. It can wait for the new mom to regain her strength after childbirth, for the parents to adjust to the new arrival, for preparations to be made, and for family and friends to celebrate. But the newborn should benefit from Baptism as soon as it is reasonable.

In some circumstances, children are older. Sometimes parents have waited for adoption. Sometimes they have household, job-related, or spiritual complications that make it difficult to arrange the Baptism right away. After a while, some parents feel embarrassed that their child has grown bigger than the average newborn seen at Baptism. The solution, of course, is simply to arrange the Baptism. An unbaptized child of Christian parents is always the right age for Baptism.

The Catechumenate

The Catholic Church celebrates Baptism two different ways, depending on the age of the one being baptized. One, the *Rite of Baptism for Children* (RBC), is for newborn infants and for children who have not yet reached the age of discernment, or catechetical age, when they can profess their own personal faith. We generally place that around age seven, but some children are ready at a slightly younger or somewhat older age. You can judge your child's status with help from your parish staff. If a child has the abilities of children who are receiving First Communion, he or she should celebrate Baptism in its other form, the Rite of Christian Initiation of Adults (RCIA). (Although the RCIA was designed for adults, it also includes the circumstance of children of catechetical age.) If you believe your child is old enough to have a basic understanding of the Eucharist, talk with your parish staff about enrolling your child in the catechumenate—a period of time given to hearing the Word of God and growing in faith (RCIA, 252). Children in the catechumenate celebrate Baptism, Confirmation, and First Communion in one celebration, usually at the Easter Vigil.

Believers' Baptism

In some Christian congregations, only adults may receive Baptism, but the Catholic Church encourages the Baptism of infants. Sometimes family members or friends from another church frown on baptizing infants because they accept only the Baptism of adults, sometimes called "believers' Baptism." Although we respect the religious preferences of others, we stand strong in our commitment to baptize young children.

The disagreement arises over whether or not someone who cannot express faith for themselves should be baptized. Catholics believe that infant Baptism depends on the faith of the Church, not just on the faith of the individual. Parents, godparents, and the whole community will surround a child with care. Through their profession of faith, children may receive the grace of Baptism.

Infant Baptism can be documented as far back as the early third century, and it probably existed earlier. After all, Jesus himself invited little children to come to him (Mark 10:14–15, Matthew 19:14–15, and Luke 18:16–17). After his Resurrection, several individuals were baptized together with their households: Stephanas in 1 Corinthians 1:16; Lydia in Acts of the Apostles 16:11–15; the jailer in Acts 16:29–33; and Crispus in Acts 18:8. Logically, these households included very young children.

You are already providing your child a home, a family, food, shelter, clothing, and a cultural heritage. Baptism is one of the greatest gifts you can ever give your child.

Church Attendance

Some parents hesitate to request a Baptism because they do not regularly attend services or support the local parish. If this is you, you may want to evaluate the reasons you are seeking Baptism for your child. Is it for tradition? Is it an expectation within your family? Is it a social obligation? Or is it rather a sincere desire to share the life of Christ?

The pastor may recommend that the Baptism be delayed if a well-founded hope that the child will be brought up in the Catholic religion is altogether lacking (*Code of Canon Law*, 868 §1.2). All you need to do is to show your pastor the hope that your child will be raised in the Church. So, think it through: How are you planning to instill belief and religious practice in your child? Whatever your current attendance habits are, if you now want to inspire your child to lead a Christian life, your parish wants to help.

Which parish do you approach? Some parents already have an attachment to a particular parish church because of their current attendance or past connections within their families. Even if you have no personal connection, the place where you live falls within the geographical boundaries of some parish that has responsibility for you. Call the local diocesan office, offer your address, and ask what your parish is. Go to that church so that the leadership there can get to know you.

The Eucharist is at the heart of Catholic belief. Our regular participation in the Eucharist is the most important sign of our commitment to what we believe. Several times in the rite of Baptism, you will be asked if you accept the responsibility of raising your child in the practice of the faith. If this is your intention, now is a good time to commit yourself to weekly participation in Sunday Mass. If you sense a disparity between how you have behaved in the past and what the Church believes, you may find it helpful to see a priest and celebrate the Sacrament of Reconciliation as you take a more active role in the Church as a parent.

In coming for Baptism, you reaffirm your own faith and express your desire that your child know and live the values of our Church. The arrival of your child signifies a new beginning in your life; it can also mark a new beginning of your life with the Church. Your regular participation in the Sunday Eucharist will express your faith more completely and will set a great example for your child.

Single Parenthood

Sometimes a child receives the care of only one parent. Two parents may separate; one may relocate with a job; one may have died; a single person may have adopted a child; one person sadly may have walked away from the responsibilities of parenthood; or the father may be unknown. In any event, the child may still be baptized.

If you are an unmarried parent of an unbaptized child, your pastor may ask for a fuller conversation with you about how the child will be brought up in the faith and how the Church can support you through your challenges. If both unmarried parents desire the child's Baptism, you may both approach the parish. If marriage is a part of your future plans, your pastor may help you make it happen.

Some single parents feel embarrassed about contacting a parish and going through the rite of Baptism in public. Rest assured, the Church wants to be a part of your child's life and to help you at a time when you may most need the supporting presence of the Christian community. That community should come to know your child, and your child will grow from knowing them.

Parental Consent

To raise a child in the faith requires the cooperation of the parents. In order to baptize, your pastor needs the consent of at least one of the parents or guardians.

Sometimes parents disagree on this heartfelt issue. If one parent desires Baptism and the other tolerates it, your child may be baptized. If one parent desires Baptism and the other opposes it, the Church permits the pastor to baptize, but he may seek a fuller agreement with both parties before doing so.

During the Baptism itself, if one parent in attendance does not consent to the Baptism or is unable to make a Christian profession of faith because of other beliefs, he or she need not respond to the questions of intent during the ritual.

Adoption

In the case of adoption, the adoptive parents may make arrangements for the Baptism, and their names are recorded in the parish's Baptism register. Although the Church does not forbid Baptism before the adoption is finalized, it would be prudent to wait as long as no extraordinary circumstances persist, such as danger of death. Your parish or diocese may have more specific policies in this regard.

Marriage outside the Church

Some parents who were married outside the Catholic Church may wonder whether their child may be baptized in the Church. In such a case, it is possible to arrange the Baptism.

Still, this would be a good time to talk to the pastor or someone else on the parish staff. Through a series of steps, the Church may be able to regularize, or convalidate, your marriage. Marriage within the Church would reestablish your eligibility to receive Communion and help you be a better Christian witness for your child. If your marriage is the first one for both of you, your pastor can help you through the process of convalidation. If you or your spouse has a previous marriage, your present marriage can be convalidated only after obtaining an annulment or dissolution of marriage in the Catholic Church. Annulments declare that the previous marriage did not possess the spiritual qualities previously thought to be present.

If you decide to take the steps toward having your marriage recognized by the Church, the Baptism of your child need not wait until all is complete. If for some reason your marriage cannot be convalidated, it is still possible to have your child baptized. Your pastor needs assurance that your child will receive a good spiritual upbringing in a home that values what Catholics believe.

Your Child's Behavior

Some parents are afraid their child may misbehave during the Baptism. Relax. Kids are kids, and whether they cry, squirm, yell, hit, vomit, or soil their diaper, we expect them to act like kids. Bring them in.

Your Child's Baptism

A Child's Death

Some children tragically lose their lives before their Baptism can be celebrated. In such cases, our Church urges parents not to despair but to commend their children to the loving providence of God, who certainly can offer salvation even without Baptism (*Catechism of the Catholic Church*, 1257, 1261). In these trying situations, the Church extends a message of hope in eternal life and the consolation of Christian burial. After all, God entrusted this infant into the arms of believers.

Preparation Sessions

Almost every parish asks parents to attend one or more sessions to prepare them for the Baptism of their children. Some also expect godparents to attend. It may sound like an event you would rather avoid—but go! You will often have a chance to meet other people like you; people who are raising children in a complicated world and wanting to do the best they can. You will hear about how Baptism works in our lives, what it empowers us to do as followers of Christ, how it draws us into a great mystery, and how the symbols of the rite reveal the majesty of this sacrament. You will learn more about what your parish can do to help support you as good parents and your child as a disciple.

You do not have to wait for the child's birth to attend the Baptism preparation session. After all, once the baby arrives you will have a lot on your mind. You may find the time during pregnancy less hectic and more conducive to thoughtful participation in the sessions.

CHAPTER 2

Godparents

Before the Baptism, one of the most important issues is the choice of godparents for your child. For some parents the choice seems obvious; for others it is a struggle. For everyone, the godparents play a significant role on the day of the Baptism, and they will establish one of the primary relationships in your child's life. No one knows what kind of person your child will be, but you can help develop that personality by surrounding your child with people you love and admire. Among them will be the godparents.

Qualifications

Cultural Expectations

One of the most commonly held assumptions about godparents is that they will be responsible for the care of the child if the parents should die. Although many people approach the selection of godparents with this worst-case scenario in mind, the Church does not define godparenting in that way. Godparents represent the Catholic community and pledge their support to you in raising the child (*Rite of Baptism for Children*, 40), but you may choose another guardian if you should no longer be able to care for your children.

In some cultures the godparent practically joins the family. Among some Hispanic communities, for example, the godparents, or *padrinos*, often become as close to the child as aunts and uncles—even closer. Some parents may expect godparents to take part in all family gatherings, be available for advice throughout the life of the child, and help finance some celebrations. In societies that expect family solidarity, the godparent may assume an overwhelming responsibility to sustain relationships with family, community, and Church.

But not all cultures regard godparents in the same way. Sometimes parents simply hope the godparent will remember their child's birthday every year with a gift or a card, and honestly expect nothing further.

Expectations of godparents vary from one family to the next. When you choose your child's godparents, talk with them about your mutual expectations. Make it clear what you are hoping for, and listen to their ideas. Be sensitive to what the culture is expecting, but personalize what you want for your child.

Eligibility in the Church

The Church has some preconditions about godparents too. In addition to the expectations of the culture and of the families involved, the Church adds a few of its own.

The Catholic Church expects the following of godparents (*CCL* 872, 874 §1):

- You must designate them, and they must be willing to help your child lead a Christian life in harmony with Baptism and fulfill the obligations connected with it.

- They must be at least sixteen years of age, but the bishop may establish a different age, and the pastor may make an exception "for a just cause."

- They must be Catholics who are baptized and confirmed, and have received First Communion (note that Confirmation is required for being a godparent).
- They must lead a life "in harmony with the faith and the role to be undertaken."
- They must not be bound by any imposed or declared penalty under Church law.
- They must be someone besides the child's parents.

Furthermore, the liturgy of Baptism will expect the following:

- Godparents will answer this question affirmatively: "Are you ready to help these parents in their duty as Christian mothers and fathers?"
- They will renew their Baptismal vows, renouncing Satan and professing their faith in our Creed.
- They may assist in lighting the child's candle.

These are the basics. Universally the Church does not expect anything more. There is nothing in the liturgy or law of the Church requiring that godparents show up for birthday parties, send cards, make regular phone calls, or develop a loving relationship with the child, although all these would be praiseworthy godparent activities.

The Church prefers that the godparent at Baptism serve again as the sponsor at Confirmation (*Order of Confirmation*, 5). Because Confirmation generally follows infant Baptism by some years, godparents should sustain a relationship with the child and the family throughout that time.

The Church expects you to make this choice for your child. If someone offers or even begs to be the godparent, make sure that this is the best person before you say yes.

In years past the Church said a godparent contracted a "spiritual relationship" with the one being baptized, making it impossible for them to enter marriage with each other. That is no longer the case.

Dilemmas

The godparent relationship carries much weight. Coming at the very beginning of the child's life, the decision may bring some anxiety. Parents face many dilemmas in making the right choice. Here are some frequent concerns:

Marriage outside the Church

May a Catholic in an irregular marriage serve as a godparent? The Church expects a godparent to "lead a life in harmony with the faith and the role to be undertaken" (*Code of Canon Law*, 874 §1.3) and "not be bound by any canonical penalty legitimately imposed or declared" (874 §1.4). These phrases do not absolutely exclude everyone in an irregular marriage. However, many dioceses and parishes have added the absence of an irregular marriage to the conditions for serving as a godparent. If in doubt, consult your pastor.

Church Attendance

Is the godparent expected to be someone who attends church regularly? It makes sense if they do. After all, you are asking this person to assist you in bringing up your child within the Catholic faith community. The Church reasonably expects parents and godparents to help the child "lead a Christian life in harmony with Baptism" (*Code of Canon Law*, 872). Baptism depends on the faith of the Church, expressed by parents and godparents. It is desirable that they live what they say they believe.

Some parishes may ask the parent for a letter from the godparents' parish to verify their parish membership.

Number

How many godparents should there be? One will suffice; most parents choose two (*Code of Canon Law*, 873). In exceptional circumstances, there may be none (872). The Church offers no provision for three or more, even though this is common in some cultures. In theory, several people could stand with godparents during the liturgy of Baptism, but the parish baptismal record and the baptismal certificate should list no more than two names.

Gender

What gender should the godparent be? If you choose only one godparent, you are free to choose a male or a female; the godparent in this case need not be the same gender as the child. However, if you wish to have two godparents, one must be male and the other female (*Code of Canon Law*, 873).

Non-Catholics

Can a non-Catholic serve as a godparent? No. One of the requirements for godparenting is having celebrated Baptism, Confirmation, and Eucharist in the Catholic Church. Our Church sees the godparent as more than a concerned relative or friend who encourages Christian behavior. The godparent will represent the community into which the child is being baptized and will help the child grow in that community. For a Catholic Baptism, only a Catholic can do that.

However, there is another solution. The Church only expects that there be one godparent. A non-Catholic Christian may serve as a "witness" to the ceremony as long as a Catholic godparent is present (*Directory for the Application of Principles and Norms on Ecumenism* [DAPNE], 98a). For similar reasons, a Catholic should serve only as a witness in a non-Catholic Baptism, standing together with a godparent from the host ecclesial community. The gender of the witness need not be opposite that of the godparent (DAPNE, 98b).

For a just cause, a member of an Eastern Orthodox Church may act as a godparent in a Catholic Baptism. Members of an Eastern Catholic Church—because they are Catholic—may be godparents (DAPNE, 98b).

During the ritual, a non-Catholic witness at a Catholic Baptism may perform all the parts of the ceremony that a godparent does. His or her name may be entered into the parish Baptism register as a witness, together with the name of the godparent.

Title

Is there a name or title you call a godparent, like "uncle," "cousin," or "mom"? Not really. They are just godparents.

Repeating Godparents

Can the same godparents have responsibility for more than one child, even in the same family? Yes. As long as they take seriously their responsibility and intention to help the children grow in faith, godparents may accept several children, just as parents may.

Superstitions

Is it bad luck to have a pregnant godmother? No. In some cultures it is considered bad luck for the godmother's child. But if you are really worried about such superstitions, you have not yet accepted one of the basic principles of your faith, that Christ is Lord of all.

Exchanging Godparents

If you are the godparent for another couple's child, may they become the godparents for your child? Yes. Some people irrationally fear that it cancels out the relationship. It does not.

Parishioner as Godparent

Does the godparent have to come from the family? Not at all. Remember, the Church's concern is to have someone help raise the child in the faith and represent the Church. Consequently, sometimes the best godparent is not a family member at all, but someone from your parish. Choosing a parishioner strengthens the bonds of the community's faith, puts your child in regular contact with the godparents, and clarifies the connection between Baptism and Church.

Distance

Can someone who lives far away be a godparent? Yes, and many such godparents make a heroic effort to remain connected with their godchildren. But obviously the distance puts them at a disadvantage for living the role in its fullest sense. Someone who has regular contact with the child can normally have a deeper impact and lend more significance to the role.

Proxy

Can someone serve as godparent by proxy? This custom continues to be honored. The original idea was that if godparents could not attend, they would send a proxy. They—not the parents—chose the proxy.

The Church presumes that the godparents will participate in the Baptism to ritualize their role and to indicate their sincerity in satisfying it. The relationship begins well when godparents make the effort to be present for the ritual and to establish real contact with the growing child.

Changing Godparents

If your relationship with the godparents fades or sours after your child has been baptized, can you have the record changed in the parish office? No. Like photographs and videos of the event, the parish baptismal register is a record of what happened, and the godparents' names are part of it. Those names will appear on the baptismal certificate every time you need to provide one.

Choosing Godparents

Brainstorm a list of names of people you know and trust, who are eligible to be a godparent for your child. Name as many as you can.

Now imagine that your child is ten years old. You have just cleaned up after the birthday party and everyone else has gone home. Think about the relationship between your child and the godparents. Over the past ten years, how often have the godparents seen your child? What have they done together? Have your child's godparents shared in the life of your whole family? Has their relationship with your child been social? spiritual? confidential?

From your list, who are your best choices now? Why? After you choose the godparents of your child, have them answer these questions, too, and compare your responses.

Your Child's Baptism

CHAPTER 3

The Baptism

Preliminaries

The day of Baptism will create memories for you and your family, but it will also affect the broader community. All those who share your faith will share it also with your child, so this Baptism will touch even people you do not yet know. As you prepare for Baptism, keep the big picture in mind. This day isn't just about your family. It's about church family. And it's about the human family about to hear the Gospel from a new child of God.

Baptisms at Mass

Baptisms may be celebrated at or apart from Mass. Your parish office can let you know if both options are available for you.

Once a little girl went to church for her baby sister's Baptism, scheduled after the morning Mass. After the closing hymn, almost everyone left the church, and she stood there completely bewildered. "Where are they going?" she asked her parents. "My sister's being baptized!"

Since Baptism establishes a relationship between your child and the parish community, celebrating it at Mass will powerfully symbolize that connection. Gathered on the Lord's Day for Eucharist, the community witnesses the rebirth of one of its youngest members. Baptisms at Mass demonstrate that this sacrament is not just about your child, your family, and your closest friends. It is about Christ, represented in his Body, the Church.

Private Baptisms

Some parents resent having their child baptized with other children. They prefer a private ceremony just for their child and their family. Often a parish has several children to be baptized on the same weekend, and ministers may be asked if they can accommodate families by performing a series of Baptisms instead of one ritual. However, the very idea conflicts with the significance of what is happening. The Baptism of a child happens because of the faith of the Church, the community that will offer its support throughout the child's life. The presence of other families will make that faith visible at Baptism.

Furthermore, the General Introduction to *Christian Initiation* says that, as far as possible, babies should be baptized at a common celebration (27). "Except for a good reason, Baptism should not be celebrated more than once on the same day in the same church."

Participation

Whatever the circumstances of the Baptism, participate in the prayer! Listen, respond, sing, observe silence, sit, stand, walk—join in all the activities of the ritual. Your participation will demonstrate your sincerity and enthusiasm. More importantly, it will deepen your experience of the mighty presence of the Holy Spirit at your child's Baptism.

The Appropriate Day to Baptize

Infant Baptism may take place on any day except Good Friday and Holy Saturday (during the day). The Easter Vigil is preferred for Baptism (*Rite of Baptism for Children*, 9), but any Sunday is most appropriate because it commemorates the Resurrection of Jesus. His rising opens the door to eternal life for those who undergo the death and Resurrection of Baptism. Some parishes limit the Sundays for Baptism during the year, so be sure to find out the options from your parish.

In regard to the child's age, as stated above, celebrate as soon as everyone can get there, preferably within the first weeks after birth.

The Minister

Normally the minister of Baptism is the priest or deacon of the parish. In some parts of the world where clergy are scarce, bishops designate lay catechists to baptize.

The minister will help establish the relationship between your child and the faith community. Some people prefer to ask a priest friend of the family, or to go to another parish where they grew up, where their parents live or where the parking is better. Again, Baptism offers an opportunity for you to celebrate your child's relationship with the community that is accepting the responsibility for sharing its faith. Your own parish minister will symbolize that relationship best.

The Place of Baptism

Ordinarily Baptism takes place at your parish church. We generally do not baptize in homes or at lakes. The church building represents the faith of people who will come to know the children and help them grow. Your parish church is one of the symbols of the rite of Baptism. If for some reason the Baptism is to take place at a church other than your own, you may be asked to provide a letter from your parish about your membership and preparation.

Emergency Baptisms

Everyone should memorize the words of Baptism, in case of an emergency:

> "I baptize you in the name of the Father, and of the Son, and of the Holy Spirit."

If the life of your child is threatened, he or she should be baptized without delay. If a priest is able to come, he should not only baptize but confirm your child as well, even if your child is still an infant. If neither a priest nor a deacon is available, anyone may baptize by immersing or pouring water onto your child while reciting the words of Baptism. The one baptizing does not need to be a Catholic or even a Christian. As long as he or she has the intent of the Church, the Baptism takes effect.

If the child recovers, give praise to God! You then bring the child to church for the rest of the Baptism ritual. In this case, the minister does not immerse or pour water again, but performs other parts of the ritual, such as anointing with chrism, clothing with the white garment, and lighting the candle.

If the child is in reasonably good health, it is better not to baptize as though there were some emergency, but to wait until the Baptism at church. Sometimes a well-meaning family member will assume the responsibility and baptize the child in private at home apart from the church ceremony. But a lay person is authorized to baptize only in a genuine emergency.

Prayer of Thanksgiving

Is there some ritual prior to Baptism that you could do at home? Sure. You could say a prayer of thanksgiving for your child. For example, the book *Catholic Household Blessings and Prayers* (see the list of resources for parents at the end of this book) includes prayers for the arrival of a child that you could say every morning or night if you wish. They thank God for the gift of children and pray that your child may share in the kingdom. You may then trace the Sign of the Cross on the forehead of your child in anticipation of the beginning of the baptismal ceremony.

You could also read a passage from the Bible, such as Mark 10:13–16.

The Ceremony: Its Parts and Symbols

The ceremony of Baptism luxuriates in symbols. Baptism expresses so many things about life, Church, family, and God that it needs a full range of images.

The *Rite of Baptism for Children* has collected many separate rituals that mark an adult's passage from unbelief to faith in Christ. You can still witness these in the stages of the catechumenate. Giving the name, signing with the cross, anointing before Baptism—these and other parts of Baptism for children are spread out over a long time when the candidate is an adult. We gather all these rituals into one as we bring your child to the waters of new birth.

At the Church Door

The Rite of Baptism begins at the door of the church. Your child is literally "entering the church," and crossing this threshold represents entering the community's embrace.

The Name

The ceremony begins with a question so simple, and yet so rich in meaning. "What name do you give your child? (or, have you given?)" (*Rite of Baptism for Children*, 37).

Our names become the main symbols of who we are. We use them to introduce ourselves and to write our signature. When people hear our names, they think of our personality and values.

When parents select the name for their child, they may choose one that represents some hope or desire.

FOR REFLECTION

1. Think about your own name. Do you know why your parents gave it to you? Do you feel that your name has done what your parents hoped it would?

2. The specific name you give your child will have its own significance. Have you decided on it already? How did you make the decision? Did you name your child after someone? If so, what qualities does that person have? Or did you want a unique name for your child? Why? Did you like the sound of the name? How did you spell it? Why?

3. Did you imagine your child as an adult using this name? Does the name indicate some of the hopes you have for your child? If so, what are they?

4. The Catholic Church has a tradition of naming children after saints or virtues. Prior to 1983, if parents presented a child for Baptism without an identifiably Christian name, pastors may have added a name to the one given by the parents and entered both in the baptismal register. Now the law is different: parents, godparents and pastors are to avoid any name "foreign to a Christian mentality" (*Code of Canon Law*, 855). That considerably opened the range of names for Catholic Baptism.

When the minister asks, "What name do you give your child?" state it loudly, strongly, proudly.

What Do You Ask of God's Church?

The next question you hear at Baptism is just as simple, just as significant. "What do you ask of God's church for N.?" The minister concludes this question by stating your child's name. He is the first one to use the name after you have given it publically in this ceremony.

The answer to the question should be obvious. "Baptism." But other answers may be given. "Eternal life." "The grace of Christ." Or is there something more?

FOR REFLECTION

1. Think about this question. What are you asking of the Church? What does Baptism mean to you and your child?

2. What are you asking of the people who witness this Baptism?

3. What are you asking God for your child?

4. Many answers are possible: a witness of faith; commitment to what is really important in life; love, so that the child may experience the love of God; forgiveness when the child makes a mistake; a place to come and pray; a place to celebrate Eucharist; relationships that mean something; opportunities for service. What are you asking of the Church when you bring your child for Baptism? When you hear that question in the ceremony, you are free to give your own answer. Think about that question before the day of Baptism. Decide what you really are asking. Write out a sentence or two. Prepare your response so that you can give it loudly and confidently.

After the minister asks you the name of your child, when you hear the question "What do you ask of God's church for your child?" tell everybody what it is. We need to know what you expect of us. We want to be Church for your child.

Accepting Responsibility

The minister will ask you and the godparents to accept responsibility for the religious formation of your child. When you ask to have children baptized you express willingness to bring them up to love God and neighbor. You will be asked if you understand what you are undertaking. Similarly, the godparents will be asked if they are ready to help you in this duty. Your affirmative answer is a simple response, but it signifies that you are shouldering a serious responsibility—Christian parenthood.

Once again, be prepared to speak up. When the minister asks, "Do you clearly understand what you are undertaking?" answer with confidence so all can hear. "We do."

The Sign of the Cross

The minister will then trace the Sign of the Cross on your child's forehead, and he invites you and perhaps the godparents to do the same. In doing so, the community welcomes children and claims them for Christ with a powerful sign. The Cross of Christ's suffering and sacrifice became the symbol of Christ's triumph, for through it he conquered death and rose to new life, bringing his disciples with him. The child now wears that invisible cross as many people wear visible wedding rings. It reminds us where our true allegiance should lie. You may continue this gesture at home, if you like, as a way of invoking God's blessing and protection on your child, and of directing your child's life toward the Cross of Christ.

The Word of God

The Scripture readings and the homily you hear at Baptism will proclaim the miracle of salvation in Christ. If the Baptism takes place at Sunday Mass, you will probably hear the Scriptures assigned for that day. Many people benefit from praying over the Scriptures in the days before the celebration in order to prepare themselves to hear the readings aloud. "When the sacred scriptures are read in the church, God himself speaks to his people, and Christ, present in his word, proclaims the gospel" (*General Instruction of the Roman Missal*, 29).

Listening to the Word of God helps you enter more deeply into the meaning of this celebration. God has revealed the divine plan through the Scriptures. Your family will have its place within that plan. The Word of God will be ever ready to guide the spiritual formation of your child. Reading from the Bible at home is a good way to form yourself in the duty of parenting.

Intercessions (Prayer of the Faithful or Universal Prayer)

We pray to God for those to be baptized, their families, and the entire community. This prayer fulfills the priestly responsibility we received at our Baptism to intercede for the needs of others. These intercessions conclude with an invocation of the saints. We ask everyone—in heaven and earth—to join in prayer for your child.

The Oil of Catechumens

The minister will offer a prayer of exorcism and may anoint your child with the oil of catechumens.

You hear the word *exorcism* and you might imagine something awful. Actually it is just a simple prayer. But what it invokes is something *awe-ful*. The prayer recalls the Gospel stories of exorcisms, where Jesus demonstrated power to cast out Satan. As our redeemer, Jesus also rescues us from the darkness of sin and brings us into the light of grace. In this prayer, we ask that God, who holds this power over evil, will set your child free from original sin and impart the Holy Spirit. The Catholic Church believes that Baptism frees from original sin. Prior to Baptism, we were more susceptible to the evils and temptations of the world. In Baptism, with the power of Christ, we stand prepared to fight off whatever distracts us from devoting our hearts to charity. That is the prayer of exorcism we pray for your child.

With this prayer the minister may anoint your child on the breast with the oil of catechumens. Traditionally, this represents a protective oil, like a sunscreen if you will, to reinforce the prayers of exorcism and keep away every evil influence from those who would now devote their lives to Christ. Before your child enters the waters of Baptism, this oil accompanies our prayers that Christ will bring strength for new birth. If your child is wearing a garment that fits closely around the neck, be sure to have it loosened.

The minister may omit this anointing; if so, he will still pray for the strength of Christ and lay a hand on your child in silence.

The Font

Depending on the arrangement of the furnishings in your church, you may process to the font at this time. This procession acts out your desire to bring your child to Christ, the fountain of living water. We march to the font as we

march through time, which beckons us on toward the healing rivers of our eternal home.

The font itself is a sacred place of rebirth. Part womb, part tomb, it offers new life as it puts to death all that keeps us from Christ. Its waters bring newness of life and cleansing from sin. Fonts come in a variety of shapes and sizes. The one in your parish church may be a small basin on a pedestal or a bowl large enough for Baptism by immersion.

Blessing of the Water

Observing an ancient custom in the Church, the minister will bless the water. If the Baptism takes place during the Easter season, he may use the water already blessed at Easter. On that day, water is blessed specifically for Baptism. We pray that the water may receive by the Holy Spirit the grace of the only-begotten Son of God.

Upon entering a church, we customarily sign ourselves with holy water. That simple gesture reminds us of our Baptism, when we were first brought to life in Christ by the sacred waters of a font.

Many people keep holy water at home. If you wish, you may bring a container with a removable cap to church and ask for some of the blessed water from the Baptism of your child. Many people sign themselves or their homes with holy water, praying in thanksgiving or asking for God's protection.

Baptismal Vows

As the time for Baptism draws near, the minister will invite you and the godparents to renew your baptismal vows. This provides another assurance that you intend to help your child grow strong in the practice of the faith. The minister will ask you to renounce sin and profess your faith in God. When he asks questions such as "Do you believe?" you and the godparents answer with all the faith in your heart, "I do."

The entire community may renew its vows with you. We all accept responsibility for your child's formation in faith.

Holding the Baby

Formerly the Church asked the godparents to hold the baby for Baptism. Now the parents hold the child.

This change illustrates an important shift in the *Rite of Baptism for Children* as envisioned by the Second Vatican Council. In the previous rite, the godparents' role was critical. They held the baby. The minister directed the questions to the baby, and the godparents responded. (For example, "Do you believe in God, the Father almighty?") The parents were barely mentioned at all. In the present rite, the mother or father holds the infant since parents play a stronger role. They accept responsibility for training the child, make the affirmation that they are truly asking for Baptism, supply the name of the child, and receive a blessing. The minister now directs the questions to the parents.

There are a couple of reasons why the former rite did not mention much about parents. Because the Baptism of infants generally took place shortly after birth, the new mother had often not yet recovered enough to attend. In addition, the rite of infant Baptism was adapted from the rite of adult Baptism, in which the parents of the adult being baptized did not figure into the decision for Baptism, but the godparents played an important role representing the community. Consequently, when the rites were first adapted for children, there was no model of the parents' role.

Now the role of parents is clear and strong. The rite prefers that the child be held by a parent, but it does permit the godmother or godfather to hold the child where people feel the previous custom should be maintained. In Hispanic cultures, for example, the custom of having the godmother hold the infant helps establish their bond. The rite permits this, but it clearly expresses a preference for the mother or father to hold the child so as to signify that parents have the primary responsibility in raising the child in the practice of the faith.

Baptism: Immersion or Pouring

Immediately before the Baptism of your child, the minister will ask you to state your intention one last time. You will be sharing your faith with your child in the midst of a community of believers. That community wishes to hear from you clearly that this is what you want. The minister will ask, "Is it your will that your child should be baptized in the faith of the Church, which we have all professed with you?" You should answer in a clear voice: "It is."

He will then recite the ancient formula of Baptism: "I baptize you in the name of the Father, and of the Son, and of the Holy Spirit." These words are inspired by a saying of Jesus at the end of Matthew's Gospel, where he instructs his disciples to go out and teach all nations, baptizing them. The formula can be found in the earliest Christian documents and has endured to our own day.

Baptism may take place by immersion or by pouring. Immersing the child in water more fully shows the significance of this event (*Catechism of the Catholic Church*, 1239). Baptism brings new birth. It cleanses from sin. It gives a share in the death and Resurrection of Christ. It invites a complete surrender of oneself to God. Baptism is not just a purification rite; it represents a complete change. It accomplishes discipleship, the embrace of the Church, and the promise of eternal life. It demands a big symbol so we all can get the point. Immersion dramatically reveals all these meanings of Baptism much more abundantly than pouring water.

In immersion, the minister will lower your child into the water three times. It is not essential that an infant's face be submerged. If you choose immersion for your child, you may bring him or her to church wearing whatever seems comfortable and appropriate. A few minutes before the Baptism, you may remove the infant's clothing and wrap him or her in a blanket or a towel. When the time for baptizing comes, while you hold open the towel, the minister will receive the naked baby from you, immerse the infant three times in the water, and place your child in your arms again.

Alternatively, you may have the minister pour water three times over the head of your child.

Chrism

Immediately after the Baptism, the minister will anoint the crown of your child's head with chrism.

Chrism is one of three oils we use for sacraments in the Catholic Church. (The others are the oil of catechumens and the oil of the sick.) All three are blessed or consecrated by your bishop in a solemn ceremony at your cathedral shortly before Easter each year. When you attend the Chrism Mass, you may witness the consecration of the chrism for the Baptism of your child.

Only a bishop may consecrate chrism. Chrism is a mix of vegetable oil (usually olive oil) with a perfume (traditionally, balsam). Be sure to smell the aroma! We use it only for these solemn rituals: Baptism, Confirmation, the ordination of a priest, and the consecration of the new altar and walls of a church. We use chrism with those sacraments that a person celebrates only once. After you have been anointed with chrism, it stays with you forever.

When your child is anointed with chrism, the minister will address the infant concerning the significance of the oil. In the Old Testament, solemn anointings were given to priests, prophets, and kings. Jesus, in whom the Holy Spirit dwelled, was "anointed" with that Spirit for the same purposes—to be our priest, prophet, and king. Now we anoint the newly baptized to share in that same service.

Baptized children will live always as members of that anointed body of Christ. The anointing symbolizes the respect owed to them but it also signifies their immense responsibility—to be priest, by offering prayer and sacrifice; to be prophet, by announcing the Word of God; and to be royalty, by accepting the role of a servant-leader. They are called to be disciples, to bring good news to the poor, to bring hope to the downtrodden. By this anointing, we consecrate and challenge your child to accept the implications of discipleship in Christ.

The White Garment

A white garment is placed on every newly baptized person. It clothes them in a "uniform" to make them recognizable as those who share the risen life of Christ. For that reason, the garment should be white. The minister will address some words directly to your child, inviting him or her to see in the garment a sign of Christian dignity, and to bring that dignity unstained to eternal life in heaven. For many centuries, the sound of this prayer has rung in the ears of the newly baptized. You will overhear it, reminding you of your duty to help your child keep that Christian dignity as pure as the garment.

The Church gives no further recommendation about how this garment should look. In many parishes, the child receives a bib or a stole—something that resembles a cloth more than a garment. The most obvious baptismal garment is the white gown that a child typically wears to church this day. Often this garment is handed down through several generations in a family. In fact, the Rite of Baptism suggests that the family provide the garment.

This brings up one of our most puzzling baptismal customs. When we dress children up on the morning of their Baptism, we give them the white garment before Baptism. We dress them in the very garment that is meant to be given after Baptism. Because of this, many people simply put another article (the bib or stole) over the white garment that the child is already wearing. At best this is redundant; at worst it pretends that the beautiful garment the child is wearing has nothing to do with Baptism at all.

Is there a better solution? The symbol works best when the child comes to church wearing something other than the traditional baptismal garment. These clothes are removed for Baptism by immersion. Following the Baptism, the white garment is put on the child. This may mean changing a family tradition about what the child wears at the beginning of the ceremony, but it would give a clearer meaning to this part of the rite.

The Candle

Near the font you will see the tall Paschal candle proudly aflame. We light a new Paschal candle each year from fire blessed at the Easter Vigil. When you attend the Easter Vigil, you will witness the first lighting of this candle that will stand ablaze at your child's Baptism. Then, after the placement of the white garment, someone from your family or a godparent will light a new candle from the Paschal candle, a sign that this child now shares in the risen life of Christ. The minister addresses the parents and godparents, asking them to keep the light of Christ burning brightly in the child, so that at the end of time he or she may meet the Lord with all the saints, lamp burning ready.

Most parishes obtain special candles for this purpose. Some carry the design of the current year's Paschal candle. Yet any candle will do. You may even decorate one with the name of your child or the date of Baptism. You may relight the candle for a celebration on the anniversary of the child's birth or Baptism.

Ephphetha

By far the most unfamiliar word in the baptismal ceremony, *ephphetha* is an Aramaic word spoken by Jesus in his own language when he cured a deaf man with a speech impediment (Mark 7:31–37). It means "Be opened."

From the early days of the Church, ministers spoke this word to those about to be baptized, not because they were physically impaired, but because they might have had a spiritual impairment that had to be removed. In the current *Rite of Baptism for Children* this ritual has been moved from its position before Baptism, where it assisted those about to profess their own faith, into a position after Baptism, where it prays that this infant may grow in hearing and proclaiming God's Word. The ephphetha is optional. If the minister performs it, he will touch the ears and mouth of your child while praying that Jesus may soon touch these ears to receive his Word and this mouth to proclaim his faith. The word may be unfamiliar, but its sentiment is magnificent.

The Lord's Prayer

When the Lord's Prayer is recited, the minister may remind everyone that one day your child will receive the fullness of God's Spirit in Confirmation and will share in Christ's banquet at Communion. Looking forward to that Communion and in the name of your child, everyone prays as Jesus taught us.

When Baptism is celebrated outside of Mass, everyone may process from the font to the altar for the Lord's Prayer. This procession serves the practical function of getting people to the altar for the part of the rite that anticipates First Communion. It also symbolizes our own pilgrimage, a community walking by faith toward the eternal banquet of God's love.

Blessing

The Rite of Baptism concludes with blessings for the parents, godparents, and everyone present.

Other Considerations

Besides the ritual, you may be concerned about a few other details.

Photography

You may want photographs, video footage, or a live broadcast of the Baptism. If so, consult with your parish first. Some churches have policies about what may be photographed and when, and where photographers may stand. You can help by letting the rest of the family know the local rules.

Baptism is first of all a time for prayer, and only secondarily a time for documentation. Even those with cameras are invited to join in the prayer with everyone else. If they obstruct the view of others or cause people's attention to focus on them rather than on the event, they are not helping the celebration, no matter how great the pictures look at the end. A well-staged photograph before or after the Baptism may make a more appropriate memory of the day than an intrusive shot that distracts people from the celebration of Baptism.

Party

You may be planning a get-together after the Baptism for your family and friends. A great idea! Many of the people who love you will want to share your happiness. Making time for them after the event will help sustain the joy of the day and make it more memorable. A fiesta celebrates the favor of God; some families give guests a *capia* (a souvenir) or *bolo*, a few coins to signify the wealth of God's blessings. A good celebration draws together many of our values—life, family, faith, and blessedness.

The Baptismal Certificate

After the Baptism you will receive a certificate giving you the information recorded in the parish baptismal register. Be attentive to this: your child's permanent sacramental record will always be kept at this parish church. Before your child is confirmed, married, or ordained in years to come, he or she will need an updated copy of the baptismal certificate. It will always be issued from this church. If your child's wedding takes place at another

Catholic parish, for example, the priest there will have to send a notification to the church where your child was baptized. The main information about your child's sacramental life—wherever those events may happen—will always be recorded in this parish, on the very page of the register where the staff records the Baptism.

The certificate you receive at the Baptism is for you to keep. The parish will issue a new copy of the certificate as needed in the future, updated with information about the sacraments your child has celebrated. Baptismal certificates for adopted children will be no different from other baptismal certificates. They are to make no mention of adoption and should carry only the name(s) of the adoptive parent(s). If the church should regrettably close in future years, all the records will be transferred to another one nearby or to the diocesan offices. You are establishing a permanent relationship with this parish church.

Gift for the Church

Are you supposed to make an offering to the parish for Baptism? Parishes differ on this. Some parishes set a fee for Baptism, but many families give a freely offered gift to the parish or to the minister at this time. Churches always need contributions, and your parish will incur some expenses in preparing for and celebrating this day. Parishes depend primarily upon your annual pledge and weekly gift to the Sunday collection. However, if you can make a special gift to the Church and the minister at the time of your child's Baptism, it will be gratefully received. The amount is usually up to you. How much would you spend on a nice gift for your child?

Loss

If some of your friends or family have lost a child before or after birth, or prayed unsuccessfully for the gift of a child, they may find it difficult to celebrate with you. Though they hold the same values you do, the joy of your child's day may remind them of their sorrow. Some childless couples may feel that God is punishing them—even though that is not so. Yet no words can remove their pain. As you thank God for your child, be ready to share your love with others who grieve. God loves us all, whether we experience joy or heartbreak. You will be fortunate to feel the care of God more warmly than some others will, and you will be challenged to minister to them. Their loss does not mean God loves them less. God loves us all.

CHAPTER 4

After the Baptism

Remembering the Day

When the day is over, think back over what happened. Remember who was there, what most interested you about the ritual, and the nature of the celebration. Long after the Baptism, the memories of these events will linger.

FOR REFLECTION

1. What struck you most about your child's Baptism?

2. Who was present? Who did they represent? family? friends? parish?

3. What does it mean for your child's future that those people were there?

4. The Baptism ritual involved many symbols: water, fire, and oil, to name a few. Which symbols really got your attention during the rite? Why?

5. How do you use those symbols in your everyday life, at home, at play or at work?

6. What do those symbols mean for the future of your child?

7. What words did you hear that really made an impression on you? Who spoke them? Why did they seem so important?

8. Was there a line from the Scripture or the homily that you want to remember? What do these words suggest for your child's future?

9. What else struck you? Music? Laughter? The way people looked?

10. Did something unplanned happen? What is going to make this day memorable? Why?

11. What does that mean for the future of your child?

Preserving Memories for Your Child

Because Baptism is the beginning of our Christian lives and the foundation for all other sacraments, we are always returning to that experience to deepen our understanding of the ways it empowers and obliges us to be Christ's disciples in the world. We are especially intentional about this every year during Lent, Triduum, and Easter.

You can make it easier for your child to appreciate her or his Baptism by putting together a collection of memories and artifacts from that day. You might include any photos or videos that were taken (at the church or at festivities afterward), the clothing, the baptismal candle, cards from relatives and friends, and perhaps some written or audio accounts from people who were there.

Annual Prayers and Blessings for Your Child

In the years following your child's Baptism, you can gather as a family on the anniversary of the Baptism and mark the day with a simple prayer and blessing. Light your child's baptismal candle and use the "Blessing on the Anniversary of Baptism" from *Catholic Household Blessings and Prayers*. Sign your child's forehead with the cross.

As your child grows older, share with him or her your memories of the Baptism, using the photos, objects, and accounts of the ceremony that you have preserved.

In a similar way, if your child is named after a saint, you may wish to gather as a family on the feast day of that saint and use the "Blessing on a Child's Name Day" from *Catholic Household Blessings and Prayers*.

Discipleship

Your child will enjoy the privilege of Baptism. But Baptism carries the responsibility of discipleship. Just as national citizenship has rights and responsibilities, so does our membership in the Church.

In the early days of the Church, the disciples lived in community. They prayed together, shared what they owned, learned about Jesus, and served others. These four aspects make up a good Christian life: prayer, community, catechesis, and service. Everyone who follows Christ is called to respond in all four ways of discipleship. Parents and godparents are especially called to model this behavior for the children placed in their care. So, think about this in your own life. How do you express your discipleship?

Prayer

Christians pray every day—alone and with others. Above all, we pray weekly in our celebration of the Eucharist.

FOR REFLECTION

Think about your own experience of prayer.

1. How do you worship at home and in public?

2. When do you pray alone?

3. When do you pray as a family?

4. How often do you pray with the Church? Is the Eucharist a regular part of your Sunday?

Community

The first Christians drew support for their own faith by sharing time and life with others who believed the same.

FOR REFLECTION

Think about your circle of friends.

1. Have you made good friends in your parish community? Who are they?

2. Do your friends share your religious beliefs and values?

3. How do you find support for what you really hold important?

4. Is there something you can do to become even more involved with the community of believers in your parish?

Catechesis

Even those who had known Jesus personally still made time to learn more.

FOR REFLECTION

1. In your life, how much religious instruction have you had? When was it last a regular part of your life?

2. What does your parish offer to help you learn more about our faith and to live it? What arrangements would allow you to take part in them?

3. Have you made plans for the religious education of your child?

4. What role will godparents have in your child's formation?

Service

The first disciples served the needs of others. As a parent of a very young child, you know firsthand the special care needed by the vulnerable and thus how important it is to give service to the needy and helpless.

FOR REFLECTION

1. What experiences of service have you had in your life that prepared you for parenting?

2. In what ways is service to your community a part of your life?

3. What service opportunities does your parish offer to adults and children?

These aspects of the Christian life all work together. If you are stronger in one area than some others, you can investigate ways to live discipleship more fully. That way, the words you speak at the Baptism of your child—that you are ready and willing to accept the responsibility of handing on the faith—these words will have depth and meaning from your own experience.

Parish Membership

Most Catholic parishes are formed primarily of the people who live within geographic boundaries established by the diocese. So, whether or not you know it, you belong to a parish. Parishes are structured this way to make sure everyone has a home. The pastor who oversees the territory where you live has responsibility for you.

In some ways, parish boundaries are like political boundaries. They establish a geographic unit where people can feel an identity, share concerns, and experience the pleasures and tussles of their neighborhood. A parish serves a neighborhood just as grocery stores, gas stations, schools, dry cleaners, and banks attempt to do. That makes the bond between church and neighborhood very strong. Your parish can help you meet your neighbors and share your life with them. Church is built on real human relationships, the face-to-face contact that makes friendships grow.

Although most parishes have members who live outside their boundaries, the backbone of the community is usually formed by those who live close by. Consequently, the Catholic Church generally discourages "shopping around" for a parish and encourages getting active with the church where you live. That is not meant to limit your freedom; it is meant to help you make connections close to home.

Nonetheless, some Catholics choose a parish based on location, accessibility, architecture, language, ministry opportunities, preaching, or music. If you cross one or more parish boundaries to find your parish, invest in that community as best you can.

Some of the parents who apply for the Baptism of their children are already deeply involved in their parish communities. Others are not. Many couples who come for Baptism have not spent much time at church since the time that they prepared for their wedding. Baptism is one of those moments when families and churches feel the attraction for each other. It is an opportunity for everyone to get reacquainted and to grow.

So if you are looking for a Baptism in the way you might look for a good hairdresser, sporting goods store, restaurant, or golf course, you may be in for a surprise. The Church is looking for something more. The Church is looking for a relationship. If you have not made that connection in a while, give us a chance. If you have tried and things are not going your way, tell us how we can work it out. Your parish will want to be a good companion for you, a steady friend.

A parish has much more to offer you than Baptism. The contacts you make now with your parish staff and other parishioners can create relationships that will help you throughout your life and the life of your child.

Some young families are transient. Maybe you have not yet settled in the place you expect to call "home." Even so, where you live now is your home, and the contact with your parish church is invaluable.

Consequently, it is important to register as a member of a parish. Let the staff know who you are. Come in and meet some people. Will they try to get you involved as a volunteer? Will they ask you to make regular contributions? Let's hope so. That's what Church is all about.

Remember, a good disciple does not just receive from a church, but gives as well. You have probably learned that principle in marriage or in other close relationships. In bringing your child to this church for Baptism, you are asking for the whole package. Not just a special ceremony, but a community of worship, commitment, life, and service. It is a wonderful world that is yours to share with a wonderful child.

Blessing

Thank you for welcoming this child into your home. Thank you for welcoming Christ into your child.

May God give you happiness in your ministry as a parent. May you see the hope of eternal life shine in the eyes of your child!

RESOURCES FOR PARENTS AND GODPARENTS

An Illustrated Catechism by Inos Biffi with illustrations by Franco Vignazia. Chicago: Liturgy Training Publications, 2007.
- A beautifully illustrated book with simple explanations of basic Catholic teachings.

At Home with the Word. Chicago: Liturgy Training Publications.
- An annual publication that provides all of the readings for each Sunday along with a brief commentary and suggestions for extending learning, prayer, and service. Additional questions and activities directed to families are available online. This is an excellent way for parents to prepare to hear the readings on Sunday or to further reflect on them during the week. (Also available in Spanish.)

Bible Stories for the Forty Days, stories adapted by Melissa Musick Nussbaum, illustrations by Judy Jarrett. Chicago: Liturgy Training Publications, 1997.
- In child-friendly language, the author retells forty great stories that the Church has often told during Lent. Savor these classic stories with your child, along with Judy Jarret's vivid illustrations that jump off the page.

Blessings and Prayers: For Children Who Are Beginning to Pray with the Whole Church, art by Judy Jarrett. Chicago: Liturgy Training Publications, 1994.
- Pray these blessings and prayers with your toddler or primary grade child, inspired by the lively and thoughtful illustrations that accompany them.

Catechism of the Catholic Church, Second Edition. English translation of the Catechism of the Catholic Church: Modifications from the Editio Typica copyright © 1997, United States Catholic Conference, Inc.—Libreria Editrice Vaticana.
- The official teachings of the Catholic Church for use in parishes, schools, and families.

Catholic Household Blessings and Prayers, Second Edition. Washington, DC: United States Conference of Catholic Bishops, 2008.

- A collection of prayers and blessings for use in the Christian household.

Celebrating Sunday for Catholic Families. Chicago: Liturgy Training Publications.

- An annual publication designed for families to use before and after Mass. It provides an excerpt of the Gospel, a brief reflection, a question to discuss on the way to Mass, and another to discuss after Mass. It also suggests a follow-up family activity for the day. (Also available in Spanish.)

Companion to the Calendar: A Guide to the Saints, Seasons, and Holidays of the Year, by Kathy Coffey et al. Chicago: Liturgy Training Publications, 2012.

- This book enables families to learn about and celebrate well the saints and seasons of the liturgical year.

The Godparent Book, by Elaine Ramshaw. Chicago: Liturgy Training Publications, 1993.

- A lively book that explores the special bond between a godparent and godchild. It is full of ideas for things to do together from before Baptism all the way to adulthood.

Illustrated Psalms of Praise / Salmos de Alabanza Illustrados, illustrated by Amy Ribordy Reese. Chicago: Liturgy Training Publications, 2005.

- In this bilingual book, vibrant illustrations accompany verses from Psalms 148, 150, and 104. A wonderful way to introduce young children to the psalms.

Sunday Morning, by Gail Ramshaw, illustrations by Judy Jarrett. Chicago: Liturgy Training Publications, 1993.

- This lively, colorfully illustrated book for children tells of God's love and how the Church celebrates on the Lord's Day.